KV-512-181

BULBS

FOR EVERY
SEASON

ALAN TITCHMARSH

BULBS

FOR EVERY
SEASON

HAMLYN

Acknowledgements

Cover photograph by John Glover
Title page photograph copyright BBC Enterprises

Colour photographs
Pat Brindley, pages 25, 40, 41, 43, 45; Valerie Finnis, page
53; John Glover, pages 21, 52; Tania Midgley, page 10;
Photos Horticultural, pages 16, 30; The Harry Smith
Horticultural Photographic Collection, pages 14, 18, 28, 34,
37, 39, 46, 48, 54, 58.

This book is based on *Bulbs* first published in 1984
by The Hamlyn Publishing Group Limited.
This revised edition published in 1986 by Hamlyn Publishing,
Bridge House, London Road, Twickenham, Middlesex, England

Copyright © 1984, 1986 Hamlyn Publishing
a division of The Hamlyn Publishing Group Limited

All rights reserved. No part of this publication may be
reproduced, stored in a retrieval system, or transmitted,
in any form or by any means, electronic, mechanical,
photocopying, recording or otherwise, without the prior
permission of Hamlyn Publishing.

ISBN 0 600 30710 7

Phototypeset in England By Servis Filmsetting Limited
in 10 on 11pt Apollo

Printed in Spain by Cayfosa. Barcelona
Dep. Leg. B-11519-1986

CONTENTS

Introduction
11

Every One a Winner
12

Buying Your Bulbs
14

What to Choose
19

Planting and Aftercare
22

Pick of the Bulbs
29

Index
59

Lilies grow tall and therefore look well in a shrub border or woodland setting

INTRODUCTION

Because bulbs flower well with little attention during their first year, folk often treat them like rhubarb. They plonk them unceremoniously into the roughest corner of the garden and expect them to come up and flower year after year. Sometimes they do; sometimes they don't. If your daffodils turn into clumps of grassy foliage within a couple of years of being planted then you're really being mean to them. They'll only do this when short of food and water, and they are most likely to be short of both when planted too shallowly. Always plant bulbs to a good depth so that the soil they grow in doesn't dry out. A few bulbs enjoy a summer baking but most don't, so follow the planting instructions on pages 22–24 for best results. And feed them too. When they are in flower is generally the moment at which they are making next year's blooms, and a little general fertiliser scattered around them at that time is a sound investment.

Which leaves me with just one more 'don't'. DON'T tie the leaves into pigtails with elastic bands or smart half hitches as soon as the flowers have died. As well as feeding through their roots, all plants feed through their leaves with the help of sunlight, and if you truss the leaves together, most of them will be unable to function properly with the result that the bulb is weakened and can't summon up the energy to flower. If you can possibly curb your tidy mind until just six weeks after the daffodil flowers have faded, then you can go beserk with the shears and slice the whole lot off – the leaves will have made enough food by then. But then I'm back to daffodils, and I promised you more bulbs than that. And don't think they only flower in spring; there are bulbs for every season and, equally important, for every part of the garden. Try a new kind every year; there are masses of them and most are at prices that make them some of the best bargains in the garden.

EVERY ONE A WINNER

Light the blue touch paper and stand well back – bulbs are firework plants! Inside each of these botanical do-it-yourself kits are leaves and flowers just waiting for their cue. All you have to do is supply the air, water, suitable temperature and light and hey-presto, up they come to do their stuff.

That's in the first year anyway, when you'll be benefiting from the work put in by the bulb grower. After that it's all down to you, but if you feed and tend them well they'll prove to be superb value for money, multiplying over the years so that you end up with far more bulbs than you started with.

But don't just think of bulbs as spring flowers. Daffodils and tulips will always be firm favourites as the heralds of better weather, but the summer pleasures of headily scented lilies and species of alliums are just as highly valued in my garden. Kaffir lilies and dwarf cyclamen carry on the pageant into autumn and winter, handing on the torch to winter-flowering irises and snowdrops.

Plan well, spend just a small amount and with the right bulbs in the right spot you're guaranteed some cheering flowers whatever the weather.

What is a bulb?

Anything that's fat and planted in the soil to grow tends to be called a bulb, except for the potato which is rightly recognised as a tuber. But there are four 'fat things' which serve the same purpose as a camel's hump, and this is what they are – storage organs:

- Bulb
- Corm
- Tuber
- Rhizome

A **bulb** is a condensed shoot. The stem has become a flattened base plate, the fat scales that sit on it are leaves, and these usually surround a flower bud. Once planted,

Try growing hyacinth bulbs individually in small clay flowerpots and using them as air fresheners in winter and spring.

roots emerge from the base plate and the leaves and flowers begin to expand. Daffodils, tulips and lilies all grow from true bulbs.

A corm is a condensed stem. Roots appear from its base, scale leaves up its sides and a shoot from the top. Crocuses are the best-known corms.

A tuber is either a swollen stem (as in the case of our friend the potato) or a swollen root (as in the dahlia). How do you tell the difference? The 'eyes' or shoots all over the potato show it's really a stem. The dahlia has shoots only at its top, proving that the tuber is a root.

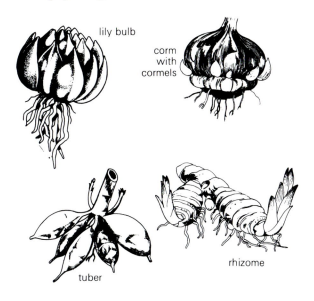

lily bulb

corm with cormels

tuber

rhizome

A rhizome is an underground stem that grows horizontally on or just below the surface of the soil. The large-flowered border iris is the commonest example. Roots appear along its rhizomes and shoots from the tips.

All plants that grow from storage organs have a resting period when they are dormant. The supply of food in their fat bodies keeps them alive during this hibernation.

BUYING YOUR BULBS

One of the first hints that autumn is on its way comes in the shape of bulb mountains in supermarkets and chain stores. Bought within a few days of their appearance in the shops these bulbs often represent superb value for money. They'll be fat and firm and ready for the garden. Buy when the bulbs have been in the shop for several weeks and it's a different story. The central heating may have burnt them to a crisp and they'll suffer as a result.

Dormant bulbs need to be cool and dry, and the person who can store them best is the bulb merchant who will

A brilliant display of mixed bulbs in spring

Plant crocuses in an old gardening boot or shoe filled with potting compost. A pair of flowery boots will brighten your doorstep.

have special sheds kept at the right temperature. You'll probably have to view his wares in a bulb catalogue, but there's no finer way of pipe dreaming than thumbing through its pages. Order early to avoid disappointment.

Greengrocers sell bulbs loose and so, too, do garden centres and nurseries. If the bulbs are sold by the pound the deal is not usually so good as when they are sold by the bag. With any luck you'll be allowed to fill your own bags, and if the bulbs are packed firmly, noses downwards, you'll end up with dozens of large chaps for a couple of pounds.

When sorting the bulbs, choose those that are firm and fat with a couple of 'noses' (terminal shoots). These will carry the most flowers. Large clusters of thin bulbs are to be avoided like the plague; they'll produce lots of healthy leaves and not much else. Discard, too, any that are soft, damaged or showing signs of fungus growth.

Some bulbs transplant best when they are growing rather than when they are dormant. Snowdrops and hardy cyclamen are cases in point. The trouble is that they are likely to be far more expensive 'in the green' and available only from specialist suppliers. Pay your money and take your choice: if you can buy lots of dry bulbs for little money it will be worth taking a gamble on their survival.

Where to plant

Bulbs belong all over the garden, not just in flower beds mixed in with the wallflowers where they can do their bit and then be dug up. Plant them:
- In beds
- In borders
- In grass
- In rock gardens
- In pots, tubs and window boxes

In beds Bulbs planted in flower beds are usually part of a timed display – most often for the spring. Tulips can be planted among wallflowers to bloom at the same time; muscari makes a good edger, and crown imperials massed together are a remarkable sight. The trouble is, from the idle gardener's point of view, the bed needs to be

Daffodils naturalised in grass are always a welcome sight and herald better times ahead

cleared once the display has faded. It's far less bother if the show is confined to part of a border.

In borders   Here the bulbs can be planted in small drifts and pockets to provide seasonal brilliance. Those that need to be dug up and dried off after blooming can be attended to without disturbing the whole display. Others can be left permanently in one spot and surrounded by plants which will distract the eye once the bulbs have faded.

In the border, as anywhere else in the garden, all bulbs that are to be left in the ground must be allowed to produce foliage after they have flowered. Daffodils that are trussed up with elastic bands or knotted into Chinaman's pigtails will simply not receive enough light to manufacture food and the flower display will be depleted in future years. Restrain your tidy mindedness and let the bulbs have full reign for six weeks after the flowers fade. Then the foliage can be chopped off without harm.

In grass   Bulbs that are naturalised in grass are one of spring's purest pleasures. Daffodils and bluebells, snowdrops and snakesheads flowering among the green-sward always have a romantic air to them. Remember, though, that like bulbs which are planted permanently in borders, those that live in the lawn must be allowed to grow their leaves for a good six weeks after flowering, and that means no mowing until then. In small gardens this can make the lawn out of bounds for an embarrassingly long time, unless you restrict your planting to the edges.

In rock gardens   Most rock gardens come into their own in April and May, when hosts of alpines start to flower. But you can be sure of a curtain-raiser before this if you plant a few dwarf bulbs among the more legitimate inhabitants. Make sure they are dwarf, though, or the foliage that follows the diminutive flowers may be a nuisance for the rest of the season. Stone sinks can be livened up with miniature bulbs, too.

In pots, tubs and window boxes   Bulbs are a must in the potted garden. Remember that tubs and window boxes are not just for summer bedding plants. As soon as

---

Leeks that are unused at the end of the season can be planted as ornamental alliums in the flower border. Their pale lilac flower pom-pons are superb atop 1.5-m (5-ft) stems.

these beauties are past their prime, thanks to the first frosts of autumn, they can be pulled out and replaced with spring-flowering bulbs, dwarf double daisies, pansies, violas and other early flowers. Bulbs can grace them in summer, too. Anemones look a treat in window boxes, and a large terracotta pot brimful of lilies is a sight never to be forgotten.

There's also winter to consider. Without the scent of narcissi and hyacinths winter just wouldn't be the same. Potted in late summer and brought in when their flowers start to show among the leaves they'll cheer you up during weeks of rotten weather.

It's very tempting to save all potted bulbs for planting in the garden, and while this shows commendable economy it does often turn a garden into a hotch-potch of weedy bulbs. If you can't resist it, see page 27.

Snowdrops growing amongst the mottled foliage of cyclamen

Small bulbs that are eaten by slugs can be protected if a little sharp chick-grit is scattered around them.

WHAT TO CHOOSE

Some bulbs like to be planted where the sun will ensure them a summer baking. One or two others will cope with fairly moist soil, but in general they are all happiest in ordinary, well-drained earth that's unlikely to become bone dry in summer.

Thanks to their stature and season of flowering, certain bulbs lend themselves readily to being grown in certain parts of the garden. This is where some of them look best:

In bedding schemes

Chionodoxa (spring)   Muscari (spring)
Dahlia (summer)   Narcissus (spring)
Gladiolus (summer)   Tulipa (spring)

In borders

Acidanthera	Cyclamen	Galtonia	Nerine
Allium	Dahlia	Gladiolus	Schizostylis
Alstroemeria	Eranthis	Hyacinthus	Scilla
Anemone	Eremurus	Iris	Sparaxis
Camassia	Erythronium	Ixia	Tigridia
Chionodoxa	Freesia	Lilium	Tulipa
Colchicum	Fritillaria	Muscari	
Crocus	Galanthus	Narcissus	

In grass

Anemone blanda	Eranthis	Leucojum
Chionodoxa	*Fritillaria meleagris*	Narcissus
Colchicum	Galanthus	Ornithogalum
Crocus		

In rock gardens

Allium (dwarf species)   Iris (dwarf species)
Anemone blanda   Leucojum
Crocus   Muscari
Cyclamen   Narcissus (dwarf species)
Eranthis   Oxalis
Erythronium   Scilla
Fritillaria meleagris   Sternbergia
Galanthus   Tulipa

In pots, tubs and window boxes

Agapanthus	Galtonia	Narcissus
Anemone	Hyacinthus	Nerine
Chionodoxa	Iris (dwarf species)	Scilla
Crocus	Lilium	Tulipa
Galanthus	Muscari	

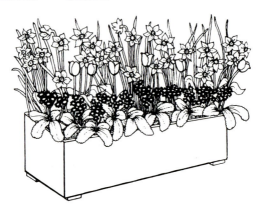

In dappled shady spots

Allium moly	Eranthis
Anemone blanda	Erythronium
Anemone nemorosa	*Fritillaria meleagris*
Colchicum	Galanthus
Convallaria	Leucojum
Cyclamen	Oxalis
Endymion	

Anemone nemorosa

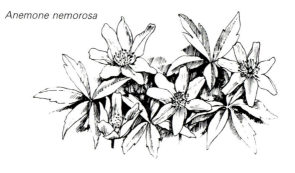

When turfing a new lawn, consider planting bulbs in clumps before the turf is laid. It's easier to plant in soil than grass.

Hardy *Cyclamen hederifolium* looks delightful in the dappled
shade beneath small trees and shrubs

Planting and Aftercare

Without a doubt the best tool for planting bulbs is a trowel. In cultivated soil it slices through the earth with ease, and although you'll have to use more pressure on turf it still makes a smart job of a planting hole. Bulb-planting tools take out a core of soil and are easy to use on light soil. In heavy or stony soil they'll make your wrists ache, unless you can find a foot-operated model.

If you're planting bulbs in grass you can either scatter them at random over the turf and plant them with a trowel where they fall, or you can lift 45-cm (18-in) square flaps of turf and plant groups of bulbs with a trowel in the soil below, replacing the turf when they're all in. This method is essential for tiny bulbs.

Depth and spacing The general rule of thumb when planting bulbs is to cover them to twice their own depth with soil. This means that an 8-cm (3-in) deep daffodil bulb will need a 23-cm (9-in) deep planting hole so that 15 cm (6 in) of soil can cover it. Bulbs planted too shallowly will dry out in summer and may flower poorly. You can allow a spacing between the bulbs equivalent to their planting depth, but always arrange them in groups, never in lines (unless you're a fan of regimented bedding).

A bulb planter takes out a neat core of soil to make planting easier

Don't worry about planting daffodils and tulips late in the season. Provided they are planted before Christmas they should still flower well, if a little late.

Planting tulip bulbs between spring bedding

When you plant tulips and the like among wallflowers and other spring bedders, put the plants in first and the bulbs in afterwards. That way you can avoid hitting the bulbs with your trowel, and prevent wallflowers being surprised by tulip bulbs pushing up through their middles.

Planting in pots   When planting bulbs in autumn for winter flowers, don't use bulb fibre and don't use bowls without holes. Your bulbs will be far happier in pots or bowls with drainage holes, and in a proprietary peat-based potting compost or John Innes No.1 with a little sharp sand added if you're feeling generous. Bulb fibre was originally developed for use with containers that lacked drainage holes, and it contained crushed oyster shell and charcoal to keep the mixture open, well-drained and sweet. Nowadays the stuff is often nothing more than peat with a few nutrients. The bulbs will grow in it, but it does nothing to assist drainage. It can be quite expensive, too. Compost is a far better bet.

Large bulbs planted in pots should have their noses just poking through the surface. Smaller bulbs can sit just below. In plastic pots there's no need for drainage material over the holes in the base of the pot; in clay pots that possess only a single hole, scatter a little gravel, or place some pieces of broken flowerpot in the bottom.

When potting is finished the surface of the compost

Grow dwarf bulbs in clumps among alpines in rock gardens and sinks.

should rest between 1 and 1.5 cm ($\frac{1}{2}$ and 1 in) below the rim of the pot.

As far as bulb density goes, you can pack as many in as you like. There's a trick with daffodils and narcissi that will fill a pot with flowers:

- Place some compost in the bottom of the pot
- Sit a layer of bulbs on the compost
- Add more compost to cover these bulbs
- Put another layer of bulbs in and cover them with compost to within 1.5 cm (1 in) of the pot rim.

Both layers of bulbs will flower at the same time.

Below: Plant daffodil bulbs in two layers. *Right:* Put one crocus by each hole of a crocus pot, then plant a layer at the top

Water the pots carefully after planting, giving the compost a really good soak. Now they can be stood out of doors in a cool place for eight weeks. This is essential. It gets the roots going so that they can support the top growth. After eight weeks, the shoots will be starting to grow. Summer bulbs can obviously stay outside; those that are being grown for winter flowers can be brought into a cool, brightly lit spot, and gradually given more heat as they grow. Dramatic changes in temperature may result in deformed or dead flower buds, so take care. Make sure the compost never dries out.

Bulbs in window boxes and tubs You can treat outdoor potted bulbs almost as though they were

The leaves of daffodils and narcissi can be chopped off completely six weeks after the flowers have faded.

growing in the earth, but do remember that you're responsible for watering and feeding them. Once planted, keep them gently moist. They'll thrive best in John Innes potting compost No.2, plus a little sharp sand.

Getting the best from bulbs

Any plant that grows really well on its own tends to be neglected by the gardener. But if you want your bulbs to keep doing well then show them a little kindness.

Dwarf irises (left) and crocuses growing in bowls

Feeding   Potted bulbs that bloom in summer (lilies and the like) should be fed fortnightly from early to late summer with liquid tomato fertiliser, diluted as the manufacturers recommend for tomatoes. It produces wonderful flowers as well as fruits!

Bulbs growing in the garden will thrive on a sprinkling of blood, bone and fishmeal. Scatter it around them just as they come into flower. As this season's flowers fade, so next year's will be made and the extra energy you provide will buck up their ideas.

Bulbs potted in autumn for winter flowers need no feeding. The nutrients within the compost will suffice.

Watering   Bulbs, more than most other plants, do like to be kept growing evenly, so try to prevent the compost in containers from becoming excessively dry. Gentle moisture at all times is what they prefer.

In the garden, dry spring weather can affect flower production, and daffodils and narcissi in particular will often bloom poorly in the year following a spring drought.

Staking   Daffodils in pots, lilies in pots and in the garden, and one or two other tall bulbs will appreciate your support. Not just verbal encouragement, but help in the form of twiggy branches pushed among them, or single canes to which they can be gently tied with soft

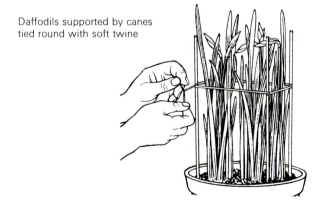

Daffodils supported by canes
tied round with soft twine

twine. Use your discretion and tie them in where you think necessary. Pots of narcissi can be encircled with split green canes linked with soft twine. Whatever you use, try to avoid that trussed-up look.

Deadheading Unless you are manic about collecting seeds of absolutely anything, nip the faded flowerheads off your bulbs to conserve their energy. They might as well use it to make next year's flowers rather than an unwanted crop of seeds.

Planting out Potted bulbs that have finished flowering can be consigned to the garden. But be careful. Think clearly where you want them, otherwise you'll end up with one corner in your plot that's nothing more than a half-hearted home for waifs and strays. Far better to ditch the bulbs in the bin rather than let them become eyesores. If you do decide to plant them out, water them and set them more deeply in the earth than they were in the pot, otherwise they'll never flower well in succeeding years.

Lifting and drying Gladioli and tulips used in bedding schemes are dug up and dried off once they've finished flowering. Fork them out of the soil and lay them somewhere like an airy shed or garage until their top growth is dry and brown. Then it can be pulled off and the largest and fattest corms or bulbs stored in dry peat until planting time comes round once more. The tiniest corms or bulblets should be discarded, unless you want to spend years growing them on to flowering size.

Propagation There are all sorts of complicated ways of propagating bulbs, but the easiest is by dividing mature clumps into individuals and replanting them. This is usually best done just after flowering. Some lilies can be grown from seed to flower within about four years, so if you're a patient gardener it's a method that will save you a lot of money. Most gardeners, though, are content to buy in new bulbs, and as long as these represent superb value for money there's no shame in that.

Make sure that all bulbs potted in autumn for winter flowers are given eight weeks of darkness and cool temperatures before being brought into the house.

Erythroniums (see page 38), dog's tooth violets, in happy combination with muscari and narcissus

Pick of the Bulbs

Adventurous gardening pays off in the bulb world, and you'll seldom be disappointed with your experiments. Try a new variety of bulb every year if you can. It will widen both your knowledge of plants and your garden's season of interest. Here are some of the bulbs that I think offer the best garden display:

Acidanthera

They look a bit like a gladioli but possess much more charm and flowers that are rather more starry. The one most often sold and grown has the very long title of *Acidanthera bicolor murielae*. Its white flowers, about 8 cm (3 in) across are centred with deepest maroon and carried on 60 cm–1 m (2–3 ft) stems in mid- to late summer and early autumn.

Cultivation   Plant the corms 8 cm (3 in) deep and 15 cm (6 in) apart in spring. They thrive best in a sunny sheltered spot at the foot of a warm wall. In cold gardens they are best lifted and dried off after flowering, but elsewhere they can be naturalised. Good for picking. A mulch of well-rotted manure in early spring, and occasional liquid feeds in the summer, will keep the plants blooming well. Propagate by division in autumn.

Agapanthus (African lily)

At one time agapanthus was considered hardy only in really warm and sheltered gardens, but nowadays, thanks to the arrival of the 'Headbourne Hybrids' they can usually be relied on as perennials provided they are planted in well-drained soil and a sunny spot. They're lovely: strappy, bright green leaves in spring, followed in mid- to late summer by 60–100 cm (2–3 ft) stems that carry an umbrella head of blue flowers. White strains are also available.

Cultivation   Plant the fleshy crowns 8 cm (3 in) deep in spring in rich, well drained soil and sun. Mulch in autumn with straw or bracken in cold areas. Feed regularly during the summer. Propagate by division in spring, though clumps can be left undisturbed for years.

Bulb fibre is not vital for potted bulbs. If the container has drainage holes use ordinary potting compost.

Allium (Ornamental onion)

It's all right, they don't stink unless badly bruised. Dwarf species are admirably suited to the rock garden and front of the border, others are knee high, and one or two will tower majestically over your head. Among the best are:

Allium oreophilum ostrowskianum flowers in midsummer

To deter mice from attacking your bulbs, try burying a few prickly gorse shoots with them.

A. christophii, 45 cm (18 in), with metallic pink footballs of flowerheads that will make you gasp when the sun shines on them. Summer. Needs sun.

A. moly, 30 cm (1 ft), yellow starry flowers carried in clusters. A good spreader. Early summer. Sun or dappled shade.

A. oreophilum ostrowskianum, 15 cm (6 in), plenty of rich pink flower clusters. Early to midsummer. Sun.

A. siculum dioscoridis, up to 1.5 m (5 ft), is also known as *A. bulgaricum*. Tall stems carry striped flowers of cream, green and purple. When these fade they turn upwards into pointed seedheads that look like Bavarian castles. Don't cut them off; they'll look a treat for weeks! Summer. Sun.

Cultivation   Plant all alliums to twice the depth of the bulbs in autumn or in early spring. They enjoy a well-drained soil that's fairly rich. Propagate by dividing the clumps after flowering.

Alstroemeria (Peruvian lily)

Although they can be tricky to establish, the Peruvian lilies are tough as old boots once they've made themselves at home. The 'Ligtu Hybrids' are by far the best, offering large, clustered flowerheads of orange, pink, yellow or creamy-white flowers intricately speckled in their throats. They bloom from early to midsummer and grow to around 1.25 m (4 ft).

Cultivation   Dormant tubers are often difficult to settle in, so go for young, growing plants that can be planted in spring. They need a sunny, sheltered spot in ground that is extremely well drained. Mulch with well-rotted manure in spring. Propagate by division of the tuberous roots in spring which can be planted 15 cm (6 in) deep and as much apart.

Amaryllis (Belladonna lily)

This is a bulb for sheltered gardens only where, at the foot of a warm wall in well-drained soil, it will send up vast shooting stars. *A. belladonna*, 60–75 cm (2–2$\frac{1}{2}$ ft), bright pink centred with creamy white. Scented. The flowers

When naturalising bulbs in grass, leave plenty of gaps between the clumps so that you can mow a path between them and admire the flowers close to.

appear before the leaves and are in clusters at the top of stout stalks. Strap-shaped green leaves emerge after the flowers have faded. They bloom in early autumn. Sun.

Cultivation   Plant the bulbs in summer in holes 23 cm (9 in deep) and 30 cm (1 ft) apart. The soil *must* be well drained but can be enriched with leafmould and very well-rotted manure. Divide clumps in summer as the foliage fades only when you want to propagate. They are happy undisturbed. Protect emerging leaves from frost with straw or bracken if necessary. Cut off faded leaves in late summer and faded flowers in winter. Water well during dry weather in early summer only.

Anemone (Windflower)

The florists' anemones are the 'De Caen' (single) and 'St Brigid' (double) types. They'll produce bonny blooms of red, pink, blue, purple or white flowers, with black centres, at various times of year depending on when you plant them. Plant in autumn for a spring show; in spring for a summer show, or in early summer for a late summer and autumn show. They'll grow to about 30 cm (1 ft) high from tiny gnarled tubers.

A. blanda, 10 cm (4 in), is a starry-flowered treasure with blooms of white, pink, blue or magenta. Spring. Sun or dappled shade.

A. nemorosa, 10 cm (4 in), the wood anemone, is available in the usual white, plus pink and blue shades. There is a double form, too. Spring. Gentle shade.

Cultivation   Plant the last two species in autumn, 8 cm (3 in) deep, in soil that's been enriched with peat or leafmould. The larger-flowered anemones enjoy soil enrichment, too. Dry soils are not much to their liking. Propagate by division after flowering.

Camassia (Quamash)

Elegant blue-flowered bulbs with tapering spires of starry blooms. They deserve to be much more widely planted.

C. esculenta (syn. *C. quamash*) and *C. leichtlinii* are the most widely grown. White forms are available. All grow

Draw up a bulb plan for your garden, marking the location of each clump. It prevents them being dug up by mistake.

to 1 m (3 ft) in any good soil and flower in summer. Sun or dappled shade.

Cultivation   Plant in autumn 10 cm (4 in) deep and as much apart. Divide in late summer when overcrowded.

Chionodoxa (Glory of the snow)

A little treasure that always does well, *C. luciliae* should be in every garden. Sprays of starry blue flowers, centred with white, arch from the glossy green leaves in spring. It grows 15 cm (6 in) high and is happy in sun or gentle shade.

Cultivation   Plant the bulbs 8 cm (3 in) deep in autumn in any ordinary soil. Propagate by division after flowering, though it's so cheap that you might think it easier to buy in more bulbs.

Colchicum (Naked ladies, meadow saffron)

Also, rather confusingly, known as autumn crocuses, which they are not. Spectacular crocus-like flowers, usually in autumn, followed by gigantic green leaves that look like mammoth leeks. Place them carefully with that foliage in mind.

C. autumnale, 15 cm (6 in) has lilac-pink flowers of modest stature. Autumn. Sun or dappled shade.

C. speciosum, 23 cm (9 in), is more spectacular with larger blooms of white, pink, or mauve and includes a double called 'Waterlily' that's pricey but exceptionally showy. Some species have chequered flowers. Sun or dappled shade.

Cultivation   Plant 15 cm (6 in) deep in late summer in soil that is well laced with well-rotted leafmould, peat or compost. Grow them among shrubs which will mask the gigantic leaves that follow the flowers. They dislike drought. Bulbs of *C. autumnale* stood on a windowsill in autumn will flower without water or fuss. Plant them out afterwards. Propagate by dividing established clumps.

Convallaria (Lily-of-the-valley)

Once the pride of every cottage garden, lily-of-the-valley sometimes gets itself a bad name because it spreads a little

Colchicum speciosum gives the shorter days of autumn the breath of spring to come

too readily. Never mind. Plant it where it can be allowed to romp and in spring you'll enjoy the sheets of squeaky green leaves that are a fine foil for arching stems of deliciously scented small, white, flagon-shaped flowers. There's a pink form of *Convallaria majalis* and a large-flowered form known as 'Fortin's Giant'. Real enthusiasts will seek out the double-flowered variety 'Plena', and also one with variegated leaves. All grow to around 23 cm (9 in) high.

Cultivation   The secret of regular flowering lies in the soil: make it rich and mulch every year when the plants are dormant with well-rotted manure. Occasional liquid feeding is beneficial, too. Plant the crowns in early autumn 8 cm (3 in) deep and 15 cm (6 in) apart. They enjoy sun or dappled shade provided they are not allowed to dry out at the roots. Propagate by division in autumn.

Crocus

Everybody knows the crocuses that flower in late winter and early spring, but there are species that bloom in autumn, too. Try *C. speciosus*, 10 cm (4 in), pale mauve, and *C. nudiflorus*, 15 cm (6 in), deep violet. Of the types for naturalising in the garden, none is better than *C. tomasinianus*, 8 cm (3 in), which spears the soil in late winter with tight buds that open into amethyst stars. Of the best spring-flowering kinds are the varieties of *C. chrysanthus*, 8 cm (3 in).

Cultivation   Plant or pot up the autumn-flowering kinds in late summer; the winter- and spring-flowering types in autumn. Plant them 5 cm (2 in) deep and a little more apart. Ordinary soil that is well drained suits them well. Pot-grown crocuses should be kept cool at all times; too much heat will dry out the flower buds. Propagation is hardly worth while; buy in more bulbs.

Cyclamen (Sowbread)

There are quite a few hardy cyclamen that have far more grace than the usual pot plant, and which are a good deal smaller, too. The easiest to find, and the most obliging to grow, is *C. hederifolium* (also known as *C. neapolitanum*). It grows just 8 cm (3 in) high and blooms from late summer into early winter. *C. coum* will carry on the display until early spring. Both have blooms of warm pink and occasionally white, and dark green leaves marbled with grey follow the flowers.

Cultivation   All relish organically enriched soil that is unlikely to dry out, and they prefer shade to full sun. Buy growing tubers if you can, or small dormant ones. Large ones have probably been plundered from the wild and may well refuse to grow after a long, dry journey. Plant the tubers *just* below the soil surface and replace them if pulled out by birds. Propagate by seeds sown in pots while fresh. Germinate them in a cold frame or porch.

Feed your bulbs with general fertiliser at the time of flowering to encourage the development of next year's blooms.

Dahlia flowers come in many forms; *from left to right:* cactus-flowered, bedding, pompon and small decorative

Dahlia

These mammoth or modest-sized plants are stalwarts of the flower garden, producing their double daisy blooms of glowing colours from mid- to late summer. There are hundreds of varieties with pom-pon or ball-shaped flowers; round-petalled 'decorative' varieties and spiky 'cactus' dahlias. Choose the ones you like with their height and colour and flower formation in mind. They'll grow anything from 30 cm (1 ft) to 1.5 m (5 ft) high. The dwarf kinds make good bedding plants or border edgers.

Cultivation   Plant dormant tubers 15 cm (6 in) deep in spring, allowing 30 cm (1 ft) between dwarf varieties; 60 cm (2 ft) between taller kinds. Young plants can be set out in late spring when danger of frost is past. Support taller varieties as they grow with individual stakes. Feed fortnightly in summer and trap earwigs (which nobble the flowers) in upturned flowerpots stuffed with newspaper and supported on canes among the plants. Dahlias insist on a rich, moisture-retentive soil and full sun. For really large flowers, remove all side buds leaving just the main central one to develop. When the frosts have blackened the stems in autumn, cut off most of the growth to leave just 15-cm (6-in) stumps. Dig up the tubers, knock off the soil and dry them in an airy shed or garage. Store the tubers in trays of dry peat until spring. Propagate by taking cuttings from boxed-up tubers in spring, or by dividing tubers at the same time. Make sure

Tulips planted 23 cm (9 in) deep need not be dug up every year but should continue to grow and flower well.

each portion has a shoot attached to it. Pot up and grow on in a greenhouse, planting out when the weather is favourable and frost is no longer a hazard.

Eranthis (Winter aconite)

Late winter treasures with yellow buttercup flowers backed by a green Toby-dog ruff. *E. hyemalis*, 8 cm (3 in), is the commonest species.

Cultivation   Plant growing plants if you can, or tubers that have not been allowed to dry out. Plant in autumn in dappled shady spots where the soil is never baked dry. Leafmould enrichment will be appreciated. Set the tubers 8 cm (3 in) deep and a little more apart. Propagate by division after flowering.

Winter aconites with their bright green ruffs should be grown in every garden

At the time of purchase all bulbs should be hard and plump with no sign of mould.

Eremurus (Foxtail lily)

Connoisseurs' plants, these. That means they're pricey and a bit tricky, but not too pricey or tricky to make them worth trying. No bulbous plant is taller or more stately, and no bulb produces more flowers. Each bloom is only an inch or so across, but the effect of hundreds of blooms clustered up each stem is staggering.

E. bungei, 1.25 m (4 ft), pink, early summer. Sun.

E. himalaicus, 1.5 m (5 ft), white, late spring. Sun.

E. robustus, 2.5–3 m (8–10 ft), peach-pink, late spring to early summer. Sun.

'Shelford Hybrids', 1.25–2 m (5–7 ft), a mixture of colours in early summer. Sun.

Cultivation Plant in early autumn 15 cm (6 in) deep and 30 to 60 cm (1 to 2 ft) apart depending on the height. The soil should be well drained but rich – these monsters are greedy. Mulch with well-rotted manure each autumn. Mark the position of plants carefully once the long, strap-shaped leaves have died down, otherwise there's a danger of the crowns being damaged by soil cultivation. Propagate by division of roots in early autumn.

Erythronium (Dog's tooth violet)

There are many species of erythronium, but the one dearest to most people's heart is *E. dens-canis*, 15 cm (6 in), with pink or white pagoda-shaped flowers and grey-green leaves spotted with liver brown. They open in spring and enjoy dappled shade.

Cultivation Plant the growing plants in spring, or dormant corms in late summer. Make sure they've not been allowed to dry out or you'll find they won't grow. Set them 8 cm (3 in) deep and a little more apart in leafy soil that never dries. Mulch with leafmould after flowering. Propagate by division after flowering if you must. They resent disturbance so you might consider it safer to buy in new plants.

Freesia

There's no other scent remotely like that of freesias: fresh and sweet and fruity. Really they are best grown as pot plants in a cool greenhouse, but specially prepared corms

Hyacinths can be staked individually by pushing lengths of stiff but fine wire down through the flower stem and into the bulb, though the bulbs must be discarded after flowering.

The stately foxtail lily is worth taking a little trouble over for
the joy it provides in early summer

can be bought for planting in the garden. The dainty
trumpet-shaped blooms may be pink or yellow or
lavender blue or white or orange. Who could live without
them?

Cultivation Plant prepared corms 5 cm (2 in) deep and
as much apart in very well drained soil and a sunny spot.

Freesias – lovely to look at, delightful to smell

Plant in spring. Stake the plants with twiggy branches, for their 45-cm ($1\frac{1}{2}$-ft) stems usually need some support. The blooms of the prepared varieties appear in midsummer. After flowering, when the leaves turn yellow, lift and dry off the corms and use them for growing in a greenhouse the following year. Their 'outdoor treatment' will have worn off. Propagate by removing and growing on cormlets.

Fritillaria (Crown imperial; snakeshead)

The 'frits' are raved over by enthusiasts who prize many exotic species that are often tricky to grow. The average gardener will get good value for money out of just two of them. The crown imperial, *F. imperialis*, 1 m (3 ft), makes an erect stem decorated with whorls of fresh green leaves

Potted bulbs last far longer in the home if kept really cool.

and topped by a cluster of orange or yellow bells that are crowned with a tuft of leaves. Late spring. Full sun.

F. meleagris, the snakeshead, 23 cm (9 in), has slender stems of grey green, narrow grey-green leaves and nodding, chequered bells of dusky mauve or white. Late spring. Full sun or dappled shade.

Cultivation   Both enjoy fairly rich soil that is unlikely to dry out. The snakeshead even enjoys boggy ground, but not the crown imperial. Plant both in autumn, the snakeshead 10 cm (4 in) deep and as much apart, the crown imperial on its side 15 cm (6 in) deep and 30 cm (1 ft) apart. Propagate by seeds if you're patient, by buying in more bulbs if you're not. Established plants prefer to be left undisturbed.

The stately crown imperial, *Fritillaria imperialis*

In small gardens naturalised bulbs can be a problem in that they take up much of the lawn. Choose crocuses rather than daffodils – their foliage is smaller and can be cut off sooner.

Galanthus (Snowdrop)

Another treasure too well known to need description, and another plant for the enthusiast who can tell his varieties apart by differences that would escape you or me. The common snowdrop, *G. nivalis*, 15 cm (6 in), and its double variety are easy to grow and cheap to buy, and they'll multiply at a rate of knots to carpet your late winter garden with sheets of their nodding ballerina blooms.

Cultivation Plant growing bulbs immediately after flowering if you can, and propagate by division at the same time. Plant the bulbs 8 cm (3 in) deep and as much apart. Dry bulbs planted in autumn will fail if totally desiccated. Happy in any soil in full sun or shade.

Galtonia (Spire lily)

Useful bulbs that bloom in late summer. The stately spires of *G. candicans*, 1 m (3 ft), carry waxy cream bells that are deliciously fragrant.

Cultivation Plant 15 cm (6 in) deep and 30 cm (1 ft) apart in spring. The soil should be well drained and rich, and the spot in full sun. Slugs love them – watch out! Propagate by division in autumn.

Gladiolus (Sword lily)

Erect and sword-like leaves of green fan out to make a background for the tall spikes of flowers that open atop 30- to 150-cm (1- to 5-ft) stems in summer. The blooms of gladiolus hybrids are available in a wide range of colours; only blue and purple are lacking. Odd-shaped flowers are available, too, such as the 'butterflies' with frilly edges.

Cultivation Plant the corms 10 cm (4 in) deep and 23 cm (9 in) apart at any time from early to late spring. They grow best in well-drained and generously enriched soil in a sunny spot. Stake the tall varieties as the flower stems appear. Feed fortnightly and water generously in dry spells through the summer. When the flowers fade, leave the plants to feed for a few weeks. Then cut off the leaves, dig up the plants and remove the new corms, discarding the old, shrivelled ones. Store the corms in

There are over 50 named varieties of snowdrop available, though some may cost as much as £10.00 each!

PICK OF THE BULBS

Gladioli come in a wide range of colours and make splendid cut flowers

boxes of dry peat in a cool shed or garage until planting time comes round again. Propagate by growing on the small cormels that appear round the new corm.

Hyacinthus (Hyacinth)

Few of us can afford to grow hyacinths in bedding schemes nowadays, but the drumstick flowers are still unsurpassed for fragrance when grown in pots for room decoration. The pink 'Pink Pearl', 'L'Innocence', white, and 'Ostara', blue, are among the best. All grow to around 25 cm (10 in) high and bloom in winter, indoors, or spring, out of doors.

Cultivation   Plant out of doors in early autumn, 10 cm (4 in) deep and 15 cm (6 in) apart. Ordinary soil and sun suit them well. For early winter flowers you'll have to pot up prepared bulbs in late summer. Others will bloom a little later. Plant one variety to a pot; mixed varieties may not bloom simultaneously. Leave the noses just poking through the compost. Three bulbs will fit in a 15-cm (6-in) pot or bowl. Keep cool and dark for eight weeks, then bring indoors when the flower buds are visible among the

Single hyacinth bulbs can be grown in special 'bulb glasses' filled with water but are best discarded after blooming, they'll be exhausted!

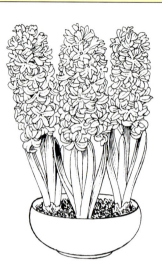

Hyacinths can be grown in bowls for indoor display. Choose prepared bulbs for winter flowers

leaves. Good light is essential for rigid stems. Stake the flowerheads individually if they look like toppling. Plant pot-grown bulbs in the garden when the blooms fade, so that the surface of the compost is at least 10 cm (4 in) below the surface of the soil. Propagation is a slow job.

Iris

The dwarf irises are a treat in the dreary winter months, opening their small but perfectly formed flowers on 15-cm (6-in) stems. The varieties of *I. reticulata* come in an assortment of blue, purple, violet and maroon shades, marked with white and yellow. As if that were not enough they are fragrant, too (if you can bend low enough!). The Dutch, Spanish and English irises bloom in that order from late spring to midsummer, carrying their flattened fleur-de-lys blooms on 45-cm (1½-ft) stems. They're blue, violet, yellow or white.

Cultivation Plant all of them 8 cm (3 in) deep in autumn. Space the dwarfs 8 cm (3 in) apart and the taller types 15 cm (6 in) apart. They'll all enjoy ordinary well-drained soil and full sun. Lift and divide the taller varieties every three years in autumn. Propagate all of them by division at the same time.

Iris reticulata can be grown outside in a scree bed or rock garden, or indoors in pots

Ixia (Corn lily)

Showy, if unsubtle, plants with clusters of flowers that resemble freesias but which are slightly more hardy. In warm and sheltered gardens they can be allowed to remain outdoors all the year round. Hybrids of *Ixia viridiflora* are most frequently grown and produce blooms that are red, purple, yellow, pink, orange or cream, usually with a darker throat. They grow to a height of 30–45 cm (1–2 ft) when they bloom in late spring and early summer, and need a sunny, sheltered spot.

Cultivation   Plant the corms 5 cm (2 in) deep and 8 cm (3 in) apart in autumn in well-drained soil. Mulch every autumn with straw or bracken to protect from frost. Propagate by division in autumn.

Leucojum (Snowflake)

Dainty relatives of the snowdrop, these plants have an

Buy your bulbs as soon as you see them in the shops to make sure they are fresh, but order special varieties from a specialist grower.

Leucojum aestivum, a cousin of the snowdrop, flowers in early summer

Lily bulbs grown in large flowerpots will survive happily for two or three years without being disturbed provided they are fed during the growing season.

equally cool charm and stems that drip with white bells during autumn, spring or summer.

L. aestivum, 45 cm (1½ ft), large white bells tipped with green. Late spring and early summer. Sun or dappled shade.

L. autumnale, 15 cm (6 in), white or palest pink bells of great delicacy. Autumn. Sun or dappled shade.

L. vernum, 30 cm (1 ft), similar to *L. aestivum* but flowering in spring. Sun or dappled shade.

Cultivation   Give *L. autumnale* a gritty, well-drained soil; the other two prefer richer, more moisture-retentive earth amply dressed with leafmould or well-rotted manure. Plant the spring- and summer-flowering species in early autumn and the autumn-flowering midget in late summer. The first two have strappy leaves; the autumn flowerer has leaves as slender as any reed. Best results are obtained with all three if they are planted 'in the green; while the leaves are still present. Propagate by division after flowering.

Lilium (Lily)

Almost without exception, breathtaking. There are hundreds of them, some with whims and fancies, others with none at all. I can do no more than urge you to grow them, either in pots or in the garden.

The best lily for beginners is easily *L. regale*, 1.3 m (4 ft), with white trumpet flowers shaded yellow on the inside and purplish without. The scent is entrancing. From nodding trumpets to upturned ones, 'Enchantment', 60 cm (2 ft), has clusters of vibrant orange blooms spotted with deep maroon. Turk's cap species dangle their flowers on tall, candelabra-like stems. *L. speciosum rubrum*, 1 m (3 ft), in white and pink, is one of the best. 'Enchantment' flowers in early summer; *L. regale* in midsummer, and *L. speciosum rubrum* in late summer.

Cultivation   Plant in autumn or spring, as soon as the bulbs are available. Plant them outside 15 cm (6 in) deep and 20 cm (8 in) apart, in groups, on a 5-cm (2-in) layer of sharp sand to make sure drainage is good. For pot growing, plant the bulbs singly in 13-cm (5-in) pots, or in threes in 20-cm (8-in) pots at the same time. Cover them

Who can resist such a lily? If space is short in the garden grow them in pots

Never plant garden bulbs in lines like soldiers; they look far more natural and spectacular in large clumps.

Plant lily bulbs on a bed of sharp sand as good drainage is of paramount importance. The scales can easily be broken off and then grown on to form new plants

with 8 cm (3 in) of compost and keep them cool but sheltered from heavy rains. Lilies love sun or dappled shade, and good drainage. Stake tall varieties if necessary. Feed fortnightly in summer. Propagation is by seed or from scales of the bulbs which can be rooted in sand and grown on.

The bright blue bells of the grape hyacinth are a familiar sight in spring. Don't forget there is a white form of this easy going little bulb

Muscari (Grape hyacinth)

The commonest muscari is *M. armeniacum*, 15 cm (6 in), which has fat little flowerheads of blue or white urn-shaped blooms held on tight heads in spring.

Don't plant bulbs right up to the trunks of trees. The ground there is frequently poor and dry and full of roots that rob the bulbs of nourishment.

Cultivation   Happy in any ordinary soil in sun or light shade. Plant in autumn 8 cm (3 in) deep and as much apart. Propagate by dividing mature clumps after flowering.

Narcissus (Daffodil)

'Daffodil' is simply the common name for the large-trumpeted varieties of narcissus, but both are indispensable garden plants always offering bright flowers and sometimes sweet scents. There are thousands of varieties, double and single, large and small cupped, in a wide range of colours from white through pale to deep yellow, and some with orange, or even salmon-pink, trumpets. On the rock garden, miniature species such as *N. bulbocodium*, 10 cm (4 in), *N. cyclamineus*, 15 cm (6 in), and *N. asturiensis*, 10 cm (4 in), look a treat in late winter or early spring, and there are many dwarf hybrids well suited to window-box and container cultivation.

Cultivation   Plant in late summer and early autumn, 10 cm (4 in) deep in beds; 15 cm (6 in) deep when naturalised in grass. Plant the miniature varieties 8 cm (3 in) deep, and all of them about 10 cm (4 in) apart. Plant in pots during late summer for winter flowers indoors.

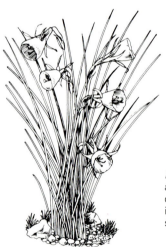

Narcissus bulbocodium, the aptly-named hoop-petticoat daffodil, is the most intriguing of the miniature species

Make a winter-garden window box with winter-flowering heathers, dwarf irises and crocuses.

'Paper White' and 'Soleil d'Or' are good scented varieties for this purpose. See page 23 for potting details and aftercare. All narcissi enjoy decent soil and a spot in full sun or dappled (not heavy) shade. Feed them at flowering time. Propagate by division of clumps after flowering.

Nerine (Diamond lily)

This is one flower that earns a tremendous welcome in the garden, for it blooms in late summer and early autumn when everywhere else is decay. *N. bowdenii* is the species most frequently grown, and its bright pink umbels of crisply corrugated flowers appear on 45-cm (1½-ft) stems before the leaves. When the foliage does emerge (as the flowers fade) it is narrow, bright green and glossy. This is a plant for sharply drained soil at the foot of a warm wall where it can rely on a little winter protection.

Cultivation Plant the bulbs just below the surface of the soil and 15 cm (6 in) apart in late summer. Full sun. Nerines prefer to be left undisturbed for years, and flower well even when clumps are overcrowded. Slugs love them. The leaves die down in late summer and should then be pulled off. Protect the bulbs with dry straw or bracken during the winter in exposed gardens. Propagate by division in late summer. Nerines can also be grown in pots of well-drained soil and overwintered in a frame. Withhold water once the leaves have died down in summer, and water once more as the flowers emerge.

Ornithogalum (Star of Bethlehem)

Easy to please and pleasing to see is *Ornithogalum umbellatum*. Its branched flowerheads carry several starry white flowers that are bright green on the undersides. It flowers in spring and grows to a height of 15 or 23 cm (6 or 9 in). You can almost set your watch by it: it closes in the afternoon.

Cultivation Plant the bulbs 8 cm (3 in) deep and as much apart in autumn in any ordinary soil and a sunny spot. Good in pots. Propagate by division in autumn.

For a splendid autumn show grow nerines in a warm and sunny spot where the bulbs can be baked in summer

Ornithogalum, the star of Bethlehem, tolerates most soils but is another one needing a sunny position

Oxalis

No; it's not that nasty weed you can't get rid of. This oxalis is one that grows from a single fleshy rootstock that never becomes invasive. There are two species, in fact, that are frequently planted in rock gardens and at the front of beds and borders:

O. adenophylla, 8 cm (3 in), has a large tuft of pale green clover-like leaves and lilac pink flowers in late spring and summer.

O. enneaphylla is similar but has paler blooms that open slightly later. Both enjoy sun or dappled shade.

Cultivation Plant in autumn just below the surface of the soil and 15 cm (6 in) apart. Both species enjoy earth that has been enriched with leafmould and peat. Propagate by division in autumn.

Don't throw away your old galvanised watering can; make some holes in its bottom, fill it with potting compost and plant up the top with bulbs.

The autumn-flowering Kaffir lily, *Schizostylis coccinea*

Schizostylis (Kaffir lily)

Spires of rich pink, crocus-shaped flowers appear when they're most welcome – in autumn and early winter. There are several varieties of *S. coccinea*, 45 cm (1½ ft), in various shades of pink, and all are worth having.

Cultivation   Plant 8 cm (3 in) deep and as much apart in spring, or in autumn from pots. They need well-drained soil and a warm, sunny spot such as that found at the foot of a south-facing wall. Protect with straw or bracken in winter if your garden is exposed. Propagate by division of mature clumps in spring.

Trap slugs around such bulbs as galtonias by sinking yoghurt pots into the soil and filling them with beer. The slugs will die a drunken death.

Scilla (Squill)

Cheerful little bulbs with short, bluebell-like leaves and pixie-hat flowers of bright or pale blue. Really easy to grow but none-the-less welcome for all that.

S. sibirica, 10 cm (4 in), bright blue flowers in early spring. Sun.

S. tubergeniana, 15 cm (6 in), pale blue flowers that open from late winter to spring. Sun.

Cultivation   Plant in autumn 8 cm (3 in) deep and 10 cm (4 in) apart in any reasonable soil and full sun. Good in containers and for pockets on the rock garden. Propagate by division in autumn.

Another blue-flowered favourite is *Scilla sibirica.* This little squill can be grown in pots as well as in the garden

Sparaxis (Harlequin flower)

Hardy at the foot of a south-facing wall in many parts of Britain, these South African plants produce bright freesia-like flowers on 45-cm (1½-ft) stems in late spring and early summer. The flowers are accompanied by bright green sword-like leaves. Varieties of *Sparaxis tricolor* are the kinds most frequently grown, and produce blossoms of a wide colour range. They need sun and a well-drained soil to do well.

Cultivation   Plant 8 cm (3 in) deep and 10 cm (4 in) apart in autumn and cover with dry straw or bracken though

A single-coloured mass of tulips provides the most spectacular show but mixtures provide a 'cottage garden' effect.

the winter in exposed areas. The plants can be lifted and the corms dried off like gladioli in autumn after flowering if preferred. Propagate by division in autumn.

Sternbergia (Lily of the field; winter daffodil)

You'd think it was a bright yellow crocus at first glance, but it's not. This is the lily that the bible begs us to consider, and any gardener who enjoys variety should plant it. It's fussy though. For some it thrives and for others it just produces leaves. *Sternbergia lutea* is its full name, and it grows its 10-cm (4-in) high flowers in autumn. These are followed by a fountain of dark green, glossy, strap-shaped leaves.

Cultivation   Deep planting in good soil suits it. Set the bulbs 15 cm (6 in) deep and 10 cm (4 in) apart in well-drained soil and full sun. It enjoys a summer baking. Allow the bulbs a year or two to settle in. Propagate by division in late summer.

Tigridia (Tiger flower)

One of the most brightly coloured and spectacular bulbous flowers of all. Each bloom lasts only a day, but

Tigridia pavonia should be more widely grown. The stunning flowers, although short lived, provide a real talking point in summer

Bulb flowers last longest in water if picked just as their buds are beginning to show colour.

there are usually half a dozen tucked up each stem to prolong the season. Three large petals provide the bulk of the display, with three smaller, spotted ones arranged among them. The tiger flower is a bulb for brilliant sunshine and a really warm spot in well-drained soil. *Tigridia pavonia* and its varieties are most frequently grown. It's about 45 cm (18 in) high and may carry white, yellow, red or pink flowers, contrastingly marked with different shades of maroon, yellow or white. The blooms open from mid- to late summer.

Cultivation Plant 10 cm (4 in) deep in rich, well-drained soil in spring. Mulch with straw or bracken in winter or lift and store as for gladioli. Propagate by removing and growing on small cormlets produced by the parent corm.

Tulipa (Tulip)

There are tulips with grace and tulips with stature; tiny miniatures and hefty giants. Pick the hybrids for bedding and for bold, brassy border displays, the species tulips for rock gardens and sunny front-of-the-border positions. The tulip hybrids are divided into groups according to their form and time of flowering. Select those whose shapes and colours appeal to you and whose flowering season comes when you most need it. If you're planting tulips among wallflowers, it's the Darwin hybrids that are tall enough to bloom above them at the same time. On the rock garden, try *T. tarda*, 10 cm (4 in), with yellow and white starry flowers held in clusters, and *T. clusiana*, the lady tulip, 23 cm (9 in), white, flushed red. Tulips vary in their flowering times from early to late spring. For container planting, the hybrids of *T. kaufmanniana* and *T. greigii* are the best choice. They're around 23 cm (9 in) high and have leaves striped with liver brown.

Cultivation   Plant in autumn (not too early) 23 cm (9 in) deep, if the bulbs are to be left permanently in the garden. The smaller species tulips will be happy 15 cm (6 in) deep, as will tulips used in bedding that will be lifted after flowering. Space the larger tulips 23 to 30 cm (9 in to 1 ft) apart; the smaller ones 15 cm (6 in) apart. Plant bulbs in pots in autumn. Keep cool and dark for eight weeks before bringing into the light. Continue to keep them cool and water with care. Plant out in the garden after flowering. Tulips that have to be lifted after flowering to make way for summer bedding should be dug up, then heeled in in a trench on the vegetable plot. There they can die down before being lifted, relieved of their dead foliage and the largest bulbs stored in a cool, dry, dark place. Propagate by dividing bulb clusters in summer. The smaller bulbs will have to be grown on to flowering size.

The starry flowers of *Tulipa tarda* are well worth growing and make a pleasant change from the familiar long-stemmed hybrid tulips

INDEX

Acidanthera 19, 28, 29
African lily 29
Agapanthus 20, 29
Allium 12, 19, 30–1
Allium moly 20
   oreophilum ostrowskianum
     30
Alpines, bulbs with 23
Alstroemeria 19, 31
Amaryllis 31–2
Anemone 18, 19, 20, 32
Anemone blanda 19, 20
   nemorosa 20

Beds, bulbs in 15, 19
Belladonna lily 31–2
Borders, bulbs in 17, 19
Bulb, definition of 12
Buying 14–15, 37, 45

Camassia 19, 32–3
Chionodoxa 19, 20, 33
Colchicum 19, 20, 33, 34
Colchicum speciosum 34
Compost 29
Convallaria 20, 33–4
Corm, definition of 13
Corn lily 45
Crocus 14, 19, 20, 25, 35, 41
Crown imperial 40–1
Cyclamen 12, 15, 18, 19, 20,
   35
Cyclamen hederifolium 21

Daffodil 11, 12, 17, 22, 24,
   50–1
   naturalised 16
Dahlia 13, 19, 36–7
Deadheading 27
Depth 22
Diamond lily 51
Dog's tooth violet 38

Drying 27

Endymion 19, 20
Eranthis 19, 20, 37
Eremurus 19, 38
Erythronium 19, 20, 38

Feeding 11, 26, 34
Fibre, bulb 29
Foxtail lily 38
Freesia 19, 38–40
Fritillaria 19, 40–1
Fritillaria meleagris 19, 20
   imperialis 41

Galanthus 19, 20, 42
Galtonia 19, 20, 42, 54
Gladiolus 19, 42–3
Glasses, bulb 43
Glory of the snow 33
Grape hyacinth 49–50
Grass, naturalising in 16, 17,
   19, 31, 41

Harlequin flower 55–6
Hyacinth 12, 18, 38, 43
Hyacinthus 20, 43–4

Indoor bulbs 18, 40
Iris 19, 44–5, 50
   dwarf species 19, 20, 25
   large-flowered 13
   winter-flowering 12
Ixia 19, 45

Kaffir lily 12, 54

Leaves, tying 11
Leeks 17
Leucojum 19, 20, 45–7
Lilium 19, 20, 47–9
Lily 10, 12, 18, 46, 47–9

Lily of the field 56
Lily-of-the-valley 33–4

Meadow saffron 33
Mice 30
Muscari 19, 20, 49–50

Naked ladies 33
Narcissus 18, 19, 20, 24, 50–1
Naturalising 16, 17, 19, 31, 41
Nerine 19, 20, 51, 52

Ornamental onion 30–1
Ornithogalum 19, 51, 53
Oxalis 19, 20, 53

Peruvian lily 31
Planning 12, 32
Planting 11, 15–18, 22, 25, 48, 49
Pots, bulbs in 17–18, 20, 23–4
Propagation 27

Quamash 32–3

Rhizome, definition of 13
Rock gardens, bulbs in 17, 19, 23

Schizostylis 19, 54
Schizostylis coccinea 54
Scilla 19, 20, 55

Scilla sibirica 55
Shade, bulbs for 20
Sinks, bulbs in 23
Slugs 18, 54
Snakeshead 40–1
Snowdrop 12, 15, 18, 42
Snowflake 45–7
Sowbread 35
Spacing 22
Sparaxis 19, 55–6
Spire lily 42
Squill 55
Staking 26–7, 38
Star of Bethlehem 51, 53
Sternbergia 19, 56
Sword lily 42–3

Tiger flower 56–7
Tigridia 19, 56–7
Tigridia pavonia 56
Tuber, definition of 13
Tubs, bulbs in 17–18, 20
Tulip 12, 22, 36, 55, 57–8
Tulipa 19, 20, 57–8
Tulipa tarda 58
Turf, bulbs in 20

Watering 26
Windflower 32
Window box 17–18, 20, 50
Winter aconite 37
    daffodil 56
Winter-flowering bulbs 27, 50, 56